ALL ABOUT  DINOSAURS

DIPLODOCUS

BookLife

by

Amy Allatson

©2017
Book Life
King's Lynn
Norfolk PE30 4LS

ISBN: 978-1-78637-046-4

Written by:
Amy Allatson

Edited by:
Charlie Ogden

Designed by:
Natalie Carr

A catalogue record for this book
is available from the British Library.

PHOTO CREDITS

Abbreviations: l-left, r-right, b-bottom, t-top, c-centre, m-middle.

2-3 boscorelli. 4-5 Linda Bucklin.6-7 boscorelli. 8-9 background - Alexandra Lande. 8br - Philll.
8m - 2j architecture. 9ml - Phill. 9bl - Fresnel. 9br - Catmando. 10 Background - JaySi. 10br -
Catmando. 11 Background - Catmando. 12 Background - Catmando. 13 Background - Catmando.
13br - aleksandr hunta. 13br - CoolKengzz. 14 Background - Aleksandr Bryliaev. 15 Background
- Catmando. 16 Background - Elenarts. 17 Background - Elenarts. 18ml - MarcelClemens. 18br -
guysal. 18-19Background - Iakov Kalinin. 19m - Marques. 20-21m Linda Bucklin.
Images are courtesy of Shutterstock.com.
With thanks to Getty Images, Thinkstock Photo and iStockphoto.

CONTENTS

Words that appear like this can be found in the glossary on page 23.

WHAT WERE DINOSAURS?

Dinosaurs were **reptiles** that lived on Earth for over 160 million years before they became **extinct**.

There were many different types of dinosaur. They lived both on land and in water – and some could even fly!

WHEN WERE DINOSAURS ALIVE?

Dinosaurs first lived around 230 million years ago during a period of time called the **Mesozoic** period. The last dinosaurs became extinct around 65 million years before humans were alive.

All land on Earth was together in one piece during the time of the dinosaurs. Over time it has slowly split up into different **continents**.

PANGEA

WHEN ALL THE LAND ON EARTH WAS TOGETHER IN ONE PIECE IT WAS CALLED PANGEA.

DIPLODOCUS

NAME	Diplodocus (dip-lo-dow-cus)
LENGTH	26 metres
WEIGHT	20,000-25,000 kilograms
FOOD	Herbivore
WHEN IT LIVED	145-155 million years ago
HOW IT MOVED	Walked on four legs

The Diplodocus was one of the biggest dinosaurs ever to live on land. It was a member of a plant-eating family of dinosaurs called sauropods.

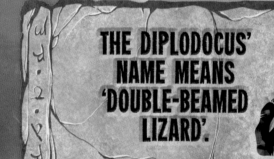

THE DIPLODOCUS' NAME MEANS 'DOUBLE-BEAMED LIZARD'.

The Diplodocus lived
145 – 155 million years ago,
before it became extinct.
It lived at the same time
as the Stegosaurus
(steg-o-saw-us).

THE STEGOSAURUS HAD FOUR SPIKES ON ITS TAIL TO PROTECT ITSELF.

DIPLODOCUS

STEGOSAURUS

WHAT DID THE DIPLODOCUS LOOK LIKE?

The Diplodocus was a very long dinosaur with a 14 metre-long tail. It had a small head and a large body.

THE DIPLODOCUS USED ITS LONG TAIL TO PROTECT ITSELF FROM OTHER DINOSAURS.

The Diplodocus also had a very long neck. It would have used its neck to reach the leaves growing on tall trees and to reach the ground to drink water.

WHERE DID THE DIPLODOCUS LIVE?

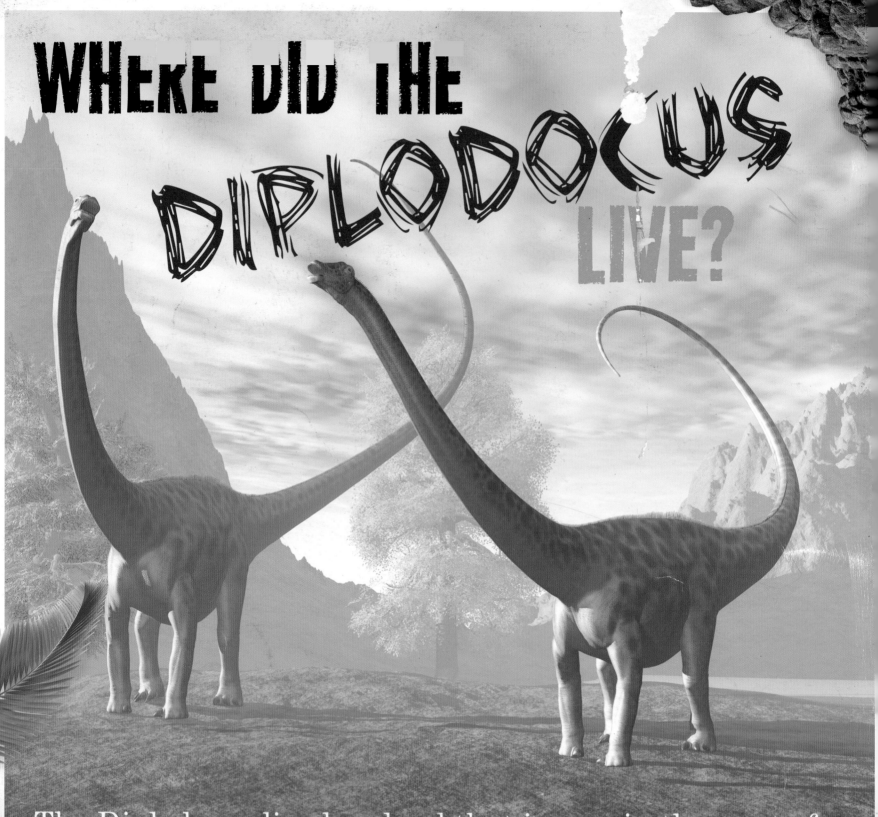

The Diplodocus lived on land that is now in the west of North America. They probably lived in wide, open fields.

The Diplodocus lived in **herds**. We know this as many of their **fossils** have been found together. They would have also travelled together to look for food, like elephants do today.

TRAVELLING IN HERDS WAS NOT THE ONLY THING THE DIPLODOCUS HAD IN COMMON WITH ELEPHANTS – THEIR FEET WERE ALSO VERY SIMILAR.

WHAT DID THE DIPLODOCUS EAT?

The Diplodocus was a herbivore. Its diet would have been made up from plants and the leaves found on trees. We know this by the shape of its teeth, which scientists believe would have been used to grind plants.

Rocks and stones have also been found inside Diplodocuses stomachs. They would have swallowed these to help them to **digest** the plants they ate.

REPTILES, SUCH AS CROCODILES AND ALLIGATORS, ALSO SWALLOW STONES TO HELP THEM TO DIGEST THEIR FOOD.

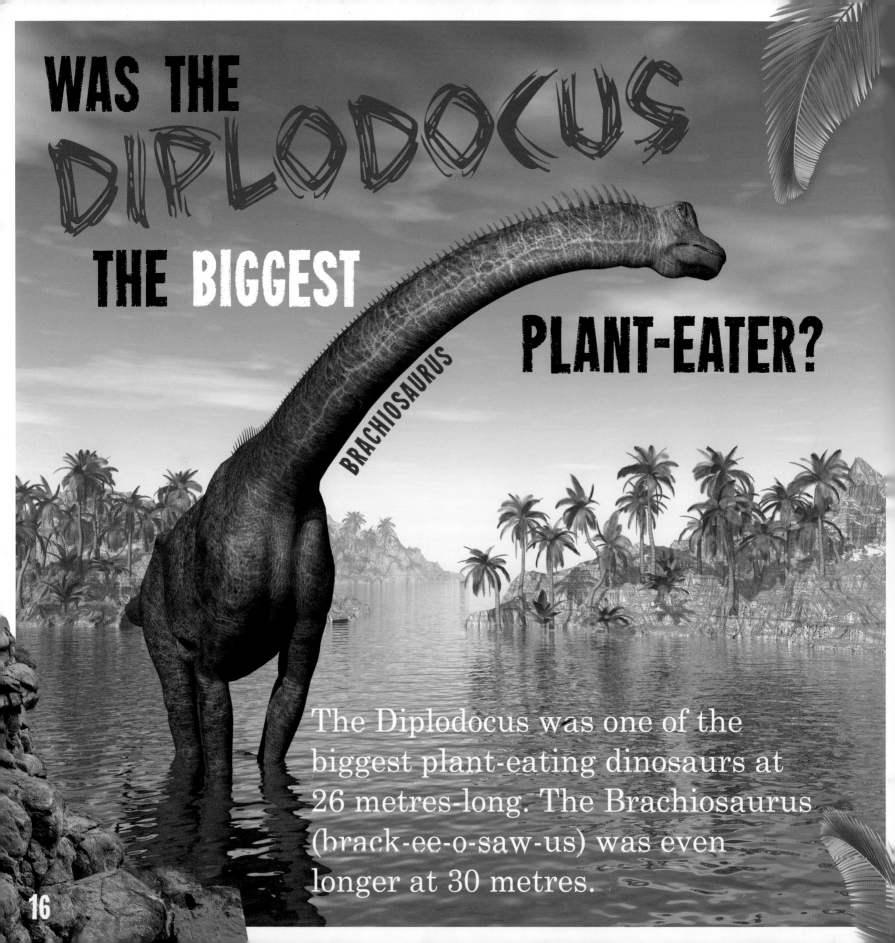

WAS THE DIPLODOCUS THE BIGGEST PLANT-EATER?

BRACHIOSAURUS

The Diplodocus was one of the biggest plant-eating dinosaurs at 26 metres-long. The Brachiosaurus (brack-ee-o-saw-us) was even longer at 30 metres.

The biggest plant-eating dinosaur, that we know of, was the Argentinosaurus (arge-en-teen-a-saw-us), which could reach a length of 39 metres and a weight of 100,000 kilograms.

ARGENTINOSAURUS

ARGENTINOSAURUS WERE 21 TIMES LONGER THAN AN AVERAGE HUMAN'S HEIGHT.

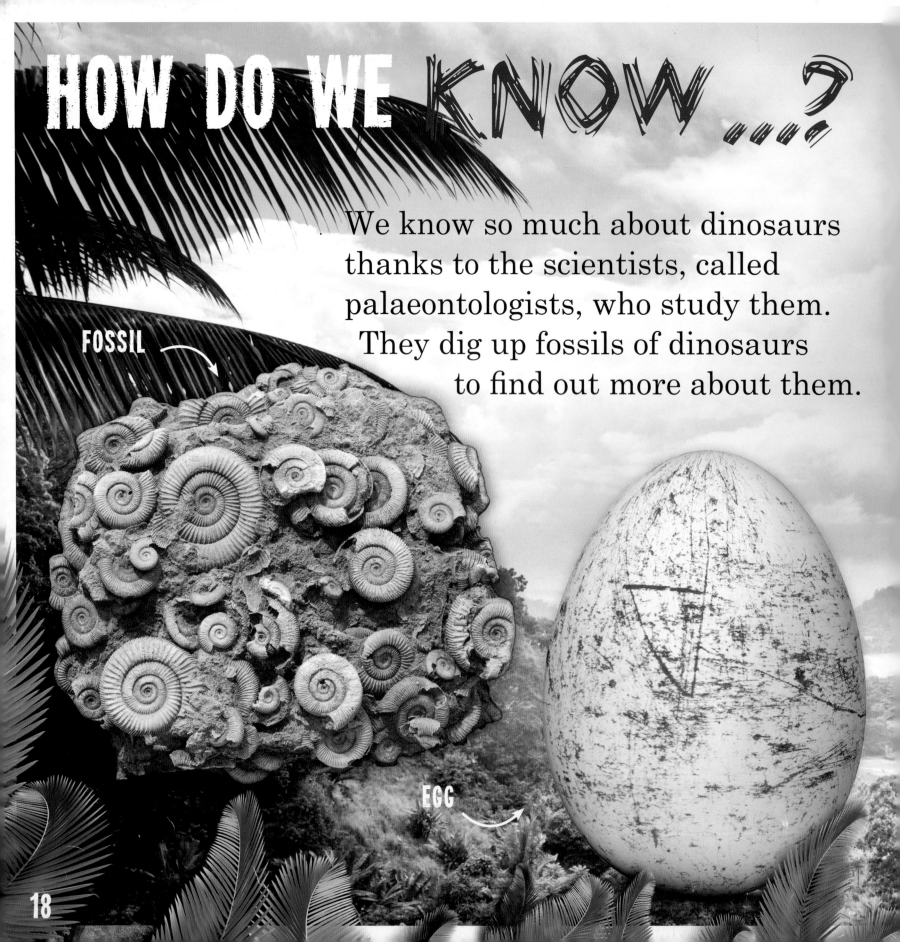

HOW DO WE KNOW ...?

We know so much about dinosaurs thanks to the scientists, called palaeontologists, who study them. They dig up fossils of dinosaurs to find out more about them.

FOSSIL

EGG

Scientists put together the bones they find to try and make the full skeletons of dinosaurs. From these skeletons scientists can often work out the size and weight of a dinosaur. We can also find out information about what it ate from its fossilised food and poo.

SKELETON

SCIENTISTS EVEN FIND FOSSILISED EGGS AND FOOTPRINTS BELONGING TO DINOSAURS.

FACTS ABOUT THE DIPLODOCUS

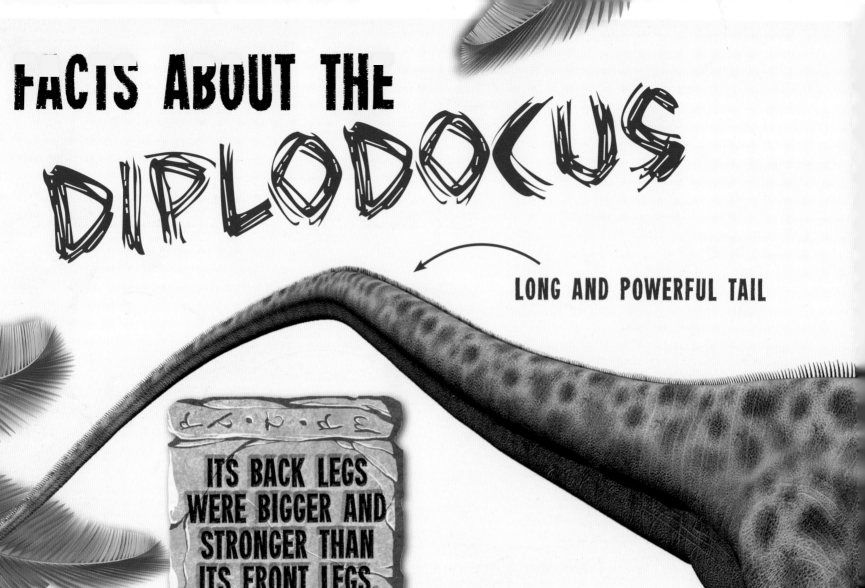

LONG AND POWERFUL TAIL

ITS BACK LEGS WERE BIGGER AND STRONGER THAN ITS FRONT LEGS, WHICH MEANT THAT IT COULD STAND ON ITS BACK LEGS TO REACH FOOD.

26 METRES LONG

SMALL HEAD

LONG NECK FOR REACHING FOOD AND WATER

ITS NOSTRILS, WHICH IT USED TO BREATHE IN AIR, WERE ON THE TOP OF ITS HEAD.

IT WEIGHED TWICE THE AMOUNT OF A TYRANNOSAURUS REX.

DRAW YOUR OWN DINOSAUR

THINK ABOUT THESE QUESTIONS ...

1. How does it move?
2. Does it live on land or in water?
3. What does it eat?
4. What colour is it?
5. How big is it?

GLOSSARY

continents very large areas of land that are made up of many countries, like Africa and Europe

digest to break down food in the stomach

extinct an animal that is no longer alive

fossils the remains of plants and animals that lived a long time ago

herbivore a plant-eater

herds groups of animals that live together

Mesozoic a period of time when dinosaurs lived

reptile a cold-blooded animal with scales

INDEX